Souvenir

SOUVENIR

London, 1979–1986

Michael Bracewell

WHITE
RABBIT

First published in Great Britain in 2021 by White Rabbit,
an imprint of The Orion Publishing Group Ltd
Carmelite House, 50 Victoria Embankment
London EC4Y 0DZ

An Hachette UK Company

3 5 7 9 10 8 6 4 2

The last line of this book is paraphrased from
Kenner, H., *The Pound Era* (University of California Press, 1971)

A CIP catalogue record for this book is
available from the British Library.

ISBN (Hardback) 978 1 4746 2230 1
ISBN (eBook) 978 1 4746 2231 8
ISBN (Audio) 978 1 4746 2232 5

Typeset by Born Group
Printed and bound in Great Britain by Clays Ltd, Elcograf S.p.A.

MIX
Paper from
responsible sources
FSC www.fsc.org FSC® C104740

www.whiterabbitbooks.co.uk
www.orionbooks.co.uk

One

Movement

After the freezing winter of 1981, with its hard frosts and clear icy twilights of intense stillness, and quiet skinny boys hunched in old raincoats, always having to walk, listening to New Order, reading John Wyndham and J.G. Ballard, and pale art school girls in the thrall of Schiele, Erté and David Sylvian, there occurred in the pop-style zeitgeist a role-playing fantasy. This took the following form and proved a sharp contrast:

A received idea of London's West End during the mid-twentieth century, mixing a concentrate of Bebop to Beat Boom modes from the late 1940s to the early 1960s and making a dressing-up box of their glamour: zoot suits, pinstripes and keychains, Alma Cogan, spivs, Julie London, Old Compton Street, *Expresso Bongo* and *The Talk of the Town*; a streetwise fast-talking cool proletarian notion of Jewish tailors, Bakelite, *Beat Girl*, pomade, strippers, Demob and Demop, coffee bars, beehives, impresarios, modern jazz, taffeta, nightclubs, Stephen Ward, rockabilly, stout, diamanté and upright bass . . . this fantasy building in exuberance, over two or three years, to embrace samba, salsa, disco, tinsel, cocktail bar palm trees – tans and tennis shorts, good times party carnival showbiz: the sound of a bright new Britain.

Occurring alongside this period costume drama of pre-Swinging London, pre-Beatle pop, meanwhile, to pursue an independent but occasionally overlapping course, was a cult of the abject, industrial, occult, transgressive, clever, days in a tower block east of Old Street, nights in Heaven or The Final

Academy counter-fantasy – which seemed the Shadow-side, confrontational, smug, oppressive, malefic, highly wrought of all that jazz samba good-times showbiz shit . . .

The Shadow-side knelt at the altar of Burroughs, Debord, Pasolini and Bataille; the Samba-side rather to Bernard Delfont.

In Kensington High Street, Soho, Covent Garden: dressing up in wilder and evermore extreme costumes, racing to outrun imitation. *'As my appearance progressed from the effeminate to the bizarre . . .'* – so Quentin Crisp had recounted, of his own youthful progress through London in the 1930s; and now, in dark rooms and basements, as shabby and basic as any rural church hall disco – here are young people dressed in knee breeches, white stockings and black pumps; collarless shirts of storm cloud grey, cheekbone triangles of cerise blusher, belted radiation suits, ruffs, robes and flounces and weird smocks and space quiffs, turbans, sashes, vertical hair, greased hair, sharp-creased US Air Force trousers; faces powdered white, plum-black lipstick, batwing swoops of silver-mauve eyeshadow, fading towards the temples . . .

Lord Byron merged with Kraftwerk merged with *Momma Don't Allow*; *Cabaret*, Roxy, Siouxsie, Bowie; dressing up for the elektro-disco modern(e); honing a fantasy of style exclusivity and high individualism in tatty West End clubs and cellars full of noise.

A few years earlier – 1976 and all that – punk (harsher, sparser, thinner, poorer, brittle in its newness) had proposed to a small group of sympathetic souls the notion of modernity itself reaching critical mass: imagine the pavement cracking, the mean corrugated iron fence falling back over the damp-blackened concrete, the white goods and deodorants and fluorescent lighting tubes and flyovers and subways and supermarkets and frozen food becoming the ancient history of a science fiction present, occupied by orphan adolescents, warming their hands by the flames of a burning television . . . And, of course, *that* was a fantasy too. Or mostly.

But somewhere in all of these fantasies, fast and hard on one another's heels, becoming a blur – punk and post-punk, industrialism, electro-futurism and new wave postmodern pop – lived and felt for real, nonetheless, by types of a certain disposition, between the late 1970s and the middle years of the 1980s, there seemed to be a configuration of existential truths, from which some members of a generation were taking their bearings.

Tottenham Court Road

Above the teeming crossroads in the shadow of Centre Point, the lowering sky presses down on the vast and chaotic pattern of streets below, squeezing the last of the daylight away, summoning night.

It is now late November 1982 – a Saturday afternoon, dark and raw. But at this end of

Oxford Street – the shabby end – the busy shops are ablaze with light: window displays, interiors and entrances, each asserting a world – all new and white, yet already worn-down thoroughfares, makeshift, scuffed and flimsy. Gloss-black mannequins, gunmetal cassette players, dancewear and album sleeves, cosmetics and electronics, books and shoes; then the blank façade of a bank and the dank yeasty smell of a pub . . . And the steady crowds and the ceaseless shuddering lines of traffic: headlights and brake lights, the beginnings of a fine sleet blowing across the beam.

Once beyond the traffic lights beside the old Dominion Theatre and heading east, the squares and mansion blocks and offices and ageing shop fronts of Holborn and Bloomsbury, Gray's Inn Road, Theobalds Road, Lamb's Conduit Street – of legal, theosophical and libertarian London, of cranks and barristers – and on, down towards Clerkenwell and

Farringdon, are quiet and deep in shadow; withdrawn somehow, as though into their own strange slumber, life stilled behind empty windows. The sodium orange of the street-lights seems to make their darkness darker, their obscurity more profound.

Here there are fewer people around – hardly any people at all. A neighbourhood restaurant on a corner, lights on but closed: three generations of the same family living over the shop since 1919; milk crates stacked in a doorway. Spearheaded railings surround the unlit squares, with their rain-blackened trees and rich scent of wet fallen leaves.

Impenetrable shadows in an alley beside the bulk of an old hotel of extravagant late Victorian design, orange brick, just now unloved, too draughty and gloomy and old; the shabby reception desk in a gleam of yellow light, the bar empty. Glimmering lantern lights on either side of a tall front door that is as black as a gondola . . .

And beyond these bookish, bed-and-breakfast districts, their blank slabs of new build, concrete and glass erratic between weekend-shuttered, still-soot-blackened Georgian squares, conjuring ghosts of bespectacled minor aristocrats and etiolated intellectuals – beyond these, the empty streets of the City's Square Mile resemble in the late autumn of 1982 more the deserted set of a grand opera: *'Huge office doors, their granite thresholds worn by weekday feet . . . stood locked . . . St Botolph this, St Mary that, alone stood out resplendent in the dark . . .'*

Beyond those, another country, purlieus of the East End proper . . . Distant tower blocks in the mist; traffic scarce; side streets, poorly lit, if lit at all, even now – everything closed, simultaneously dead and tense with emptiness; desolate, ancient, nationalist; missions and churches and philanthropic institutions, synagogues, sweatshops, estates, mean red brick balconies, light industry, market traders, Bangladeshis;

a place of flats and slums, visions, oblivion, grind, struggle, tradition, meths and boredom – unaware, as yet, of the approaching lights and construction sites, still a few years away.

For the Deep Space Industrial style is coming; will be borne on the wave of new financial industries, still in their technological infancy. And this new style – Armani meets *Alien* – will be monolithic, cold, quirky, concrete and steel, exposed service ducts, insides on the outside, glass that looks blast-proof, remnants of the past, hints of the future – romantic sci-fi brutalism, precincts as though in the service area depths of some vast spacecraft . . . Better to return to the clamour and dazzle of Oxford Street and the crush of shoppers – to the modern world.

Tottenham Court Road II

Occupying a sizeable slice of the northwestern corner of Oxford Street and Tottenham Court

Road – enough high-tech-styled, galleried and split-level retail space to seem cavernous and complex – is the Virgin Megastore, opened in 1979: a record shop on three floors that asserts itself, hereabouts at least, as the centre of the universe.

And as the first age of pop music draws more swiftly than one might imagine to a close, the total pop world of the Megastore seems imperial – pop and rock still the reigning modern form, venue for newness and risk-taking and shock and ideas and fashions and passions; enthroned since around 1956, when John Lennon first heard Little Richard.

In 1986, or thereabouts, aged thirty, pop – its principal originators, architects and pioneers having seemingly emerged – will seem to have reached a cumulative point, before reincarnating into a new phase: a phase of quotation, as opposed to innovation. Reborn in super-sized android form, strip-mining its own iconography, pop will be technologically reordered and its identity recalculated – for better or worse – for a new age. But it will no longer be the imperial cultural form, not for a while; no longer faster than all the rest, and the one from which all others take their bearings.

Meanwhile, on this dark and damp November afternoon, for those who live in the modern music world, the Virgin Megastore looks in part like a factory and in part like a nightclub, presaging the Deep Space Industrialism to come, yet still quite crude; the theatricality of the retail design on a frequency with emerging technologies. Futuristic gaming fantasies, the nearly isometric graphics of arcade video games and primitive computers.

Thus encased in a presentiment of an electronics and video-hip super-urban future pop world ('*turning Japanese, I think I'm turning Japanese, I really think so . . .*' sang The Vapors, presciently, on their hit of 1980), the Megastore proposes a universe in a shop, dedicated to the music and culture of pop and rock music: at this time, still an intricate and thriving culture of bands and trends and charts and stars and media.

Rack after rack of vinyl albums and singles and twelve-inch singles and cassettes (we are pre-CD at present); a café (club sandwiches and a new craze: cappuccino), a book and magazine department; Walkman personal stereo sets (which are the *punctum* of the pop zeitgeist in late 1982) and their accessories; a video wall of black-cased monitors . . .

The common denominator of the Megastore's assertion of a Pop Universe is electricity and electronics – domestic computers and digital technologies are on the horizon but still exotic in UK 1982; while in the recording studio, sequencers, samplers, keyboards and drum machines (including notably the LM-1 Drum Computer (aka Linn drum machine), the Synclavier II, EDP Wasp and Fairlight CMI) are enabling a new sound that is taken to be the modern sound and the sound of modernity.

And thus from these developments, electronics, machine music and percussion technology, in instrumentation and production, are the current pop cultural fetish: not just the musical medium – tinny shimmer, slap-funk guitar, boom-echo drums – but the aesthetic and electro-expressionist language of the post-punk new pop direction, implying futurism and alienation, yet super-danceable, and bending all the while towards the theatricality of the Bebop to Beat Boom style revival. A present age made of the future and the past, not the immediate.

Pop in 1982 expresses futurism, while its digital technology is still in its infancy; pop loves the machine, but looks back to the toppermost of the poppermost. What's the date again? 1962 or twenty years on? Here is a promo on the Megastore video wall, jumping into life, which may help.

'WHAT!'

The track begins with a fast sequence of sharp beats – like a robot hitting a biscuit tin, calling our attention – then an electric piano; the introductory notes are simplistic, thin and tinny, with a watery shimmer. On the video wall we see a repeated image of Marilyn Monroe in the style of a Warhol portrait. (Warhol, in this context, at this time, is synonymous with repetition, which in turn is fashionably synonymous with becoming a machine-like, cold, impersonal, auto-replicating futuristic robot-human – a default position in early '80s pop. Are 'friends' electric?)

In a succession of quick edits, four 'Marilyns' become three, three become two and two become one. Warhol is the presiding deity of the new machine pop and more besides – alienation, glamour, sex, fame, money, commodity and branding as art, boredom and repetition . . . The equation Pop = Sex × Mass Production is immediately in play.

And so the portrait comes to life and Marilyn gives us a saucy wink – coinciding with the introduction of a drum machine beat: a dulled thud, topped with a high-hat, this underpinned by a deeper, distinctively industrial, timekeeping semi-drone.

Within its opening few bars, the track is declared machine music adapting to '60s pop; the electric piano top notes play a higher melody, gathering a sci-fi theremin space-music sense of orbital flight – it's an instantly compelling, foot-tapping combination. We might remember the early days of pop media, David Jacobs on *Juke Box Jury* and a panel member gravely stating of a new release: 'It's got a good beat. It ought to be a hit.'

The world of the song and its performers opens up on the Megastore video wall. It's the duo Soft Cell, from Leeds – Marc Almond and Dave Ball – playing their version of the Melinda Marx pop hit 'What', famously covered by Judy Street in 1968 and subsequently a Northern Soul dance favourite.

The elfin male singer, Marc, is dressed in black trousers, singlet and a heavy, industrial/tribal-looking necklace; he dances with lithe energy: loose, snappy confidence, acting out gestures, flipping his narrow hips, flicking his bare arms up and across, suddenly crouching, occasionally twisting, always on the move. He has a pale face, almost white, looking up towards the camera, his big soulful eyes lined with kohl and seeming to shine in supplication. With his dark curly hair and somewhat exotic countenance, he might be the adolescent servant of some dissolute Roman god . . . *Satyricon* in Old Compton Street. His tenor voice is strong, confident, rising to the luxuriant emotion of the chorus and hook line: *'Oh baby, what can I do when I still love you . . .'*

The video has been musically and visually conceived as a flip Pop art statement to showcase

Northern Soul reworked as new pop futurism. So when the camera pulls back we see that the song is being performed within the visual puns of a total Op and Pop art *mise-en-scène*. The floor and backdrop comprise a single vast reproduction of Bridget Riley's *Movement in Squares* (1961), albeit turned on its side; superimposed on this is Roy Lichtenstein's *Whaam!* (1963) – the wording of the comic book exclamation that gives the painting its drama, focusing its Pop dynamism, now changed from 'WHAAM!' to 'WHAT!' (Soft Cell having added an exuberant Pop exclamation mark to the original title).

The camera swings with the northern ballroom, robot fairground swirl of the song, and we see that a second keyboard is being played by a Marilyn impersonator, dressed in full *Seven Year Itch* white, and giving her come-hither, teasing pouted smile to the passing lens. And the Pop art references keep coming: two boyish female go-go dancers, really going for it, wearing neo-Yves

Saint Laurent plastic minidresses printed with Mondrian-style abstraction; two other young women, fetish-dressed in black PVC, enacting Allen Jones's controversial *Hatstand* and *Table* sculptures from 1969. We glimpse Coke cans with 'What' printed on them, and the word 'WHAT' depicted in the vivid colour-contrast alphabet motif of Robert Indiana's *LOVE* (1970).

In the midst of all this, Dave chucks Marc a hat and he dances over to a sofa where the pop chanteuse Mari Wilson – wearing an extravagant, early '60s *Talk of the Town*-era ball gown and beehive hair-do – awaits him. He hits the punchline of the track: '*We can fall in love over and over and over and over again*', as the camera zooms swiftly in and out of close-up on his intent face – and the art-minded might be forgiven for thinking that this is a further reference to Warhol, and his claim to want to do the same thing, repeatedly, mechanically.

Mari, suddenly possessed it seems by the ghost of Yootha Joyce, gives a long-suffering glance heavenwards, before allowing Marc to escort her, with gentlemanly courtesy, towards the centre of the set.

Soft Cell, however electronic, were bred of rainy old England; just as Ziggy Stardust (so Bowie himself remarked) contained more than a drop of Woolworths; and Trojan and Leigh Bowery − exhibitionist clubbers like brick-layers with green faces or Indian deities by way of Boots 17 − will seem to have as much to do with crisps as loving the alien.

Which sharpened the edge of these things: a vital coarseness adding muscle and inten-sity, deepening and validating the weird-ness, connecting to the sweat, mechanics and showbiz graft of rock and roll, repudiating artiness or paraded cleverness (although much cleverness, of a different kind − strategic, cre-ative and intuitive − was involved) and other such enemies of promise.

The House of Glam was already shot through with rising damp, and then Soft Cell moved in. Their hit of the previous year, 'Bedsitter' – swinging, nervy, with the deep-sea drone industrial backbeat – seemed bred from the damp quilt and gas fire domestic claustrophobia and soul-corroding meanness of rented digs in UK kitchen sink cinema circa 1961 (wet Sunday afternoon; man turns up raincoat collar, ignores shivering peroxide blonde girlfriend, stares at distant viaduct: 'I hate this town') in which bedroom was just an anagram for boredom and everywhere smelt of escaping gas. The ghosts of Jo and Geoffrey Ingram come down from Salford to haunt cold houses in Wood Green and Whitechapel.

Meanwhile, on the set of 'What!' – a figure dressed as Warhol himself appears in the video, in leather jacket and silver fright wig, taking photographs of all the Maitresse PVC Go-Go Girls and Allen Jones fetish furniture made flesh. The camera pulls back further (in the directorial style of Jean-Luc Godard) to reveal the set and the crew of the video – and

Marc dances towards us, along the tracks, past the crew, out of the clever-a-go-go Pop art world of the video, and, we surmise, into the endless romance of the sleazy city's seedy streets . . . To where?

Tottenham Court Road III – Going Underground

Let us pretend that Marc Almond has danced right off the video wall in the Virgin Megastore, this cold and damp late afternoon in November 1982, and out of the store and across the eastern end of Oxford Street to find himself beside the small newsagent and tobacconist's stand that in those days was set into the wall beside the entrance to Tottenham Court Road Underground station. Here he would have to Keep Left as he danced down the dirty steps towards an odoriferous curve of subway that leads to the central booking hall, ticket barriers and escalators of the station.

In grimy old London he was making a journey, as it transpired, from post-punk to postmodernity. Had he continued, and ascended a further short flight of steps, he would have found himself in another, darker subway, far more odoriferous and much frequented by homeless people, in which was located one of London's few gyms. This being the winter of 1982, the times are still pre-body-consciousness, as well as pre-digital and pre-ironic. Even Soft Cell's cover of 'What', however artfully styled and recast for electro-dance, comes across as glorious Pop homage as opposed to arch pastiche.

Emerging the other side, on the eastern side of Charing Cross Road (home, then, to St Martin's School of Art, artist-polymath Derek Jarman, and Ian Shipley's art history bookshop, whose window display for Jarman's film diary and memoir *Dancing Ledge*, in 1984, will resemble a Neo-Romantic Voodoo Shrine, replete with human skull), Marc would be facing the old

Astoria theatre – soon to be refurbished as a thriving music venue – and standing with his back to New Oxford Street, a block northwards of which stood the Y.M.C.A. . . . in the basement of which new industrial noise assault bands, the electronic avant-garde and occultist funkateers such as Throbbing Gristle, S.P.K. (aka 'System Planning Korporation'/'Surgical Penis Klinic'/'Selective Pornography Kontrol') Cabaret Voltaire, This Heat, Lemon Kittens, Clock DVA, 23 Skidoo and Rema-Rema could be discerned in the darkness.

But at this time, in this part of London, quite suddenly, it feels as though the very atmosphere in the streets is about to break free of what seemed to be the monotony and chill of the late 1970s. A glance at the television adaptation (like the Megastore, made in 1979) of John Le Carré's novel of late Cold War espionage, *Tinker Tailor Soldier Spy*, is coldly articulate of the capital's atmosphere and appearance – an ill, exhausted meanness – in the year Margaret

Thatcher was elected prime minister.

Cambridge Circus appears almost as run-down, surly and sourly populated as the Eastern European cities that the British spies of Le Carré's 'Circus' are infiltrating; professional men of early middle age look prematurely aged, saggy jowled, hyper-tensile; their lumpy-haired juniors gone to seed already.

A shot of two suited men talking in a poorly lit government office looks like a bad photograph of a painting by Francis Bacon: dun and cream; light bulb dimly pinkish gleaming; intimation of mean frame of office cubicle; male humans as though twisted and crippled inside.

And beyond? Fags and instant coffee; tepid alcohol − the stale taste of too much; boxy brown cars, crimson flock wallpaper; rain; depressing dessert trolley; bottles of gold top. And so it was.

By the same token, the London streets on which the first two seasons of Thames

Television's *The Sweeney* were filmed in 1975 seem in the clutches of an older era still – a worn-out shot at modernity in the midst of urban dereliction; menace or boredom like stagnant pools; Transit vans and watery Scotch, broken-down tower blocks, ripped-out bathroom fittings, dripping lock-ups and bedsit art nouveau – the ubiquitous corrugated iron fly-posted with (for instance) announcements for 'An Evening with Fripp and Eno' at the London Palladium, and Welsh rockers Man at the Roundhouse.

D.I. Regan and Detective Sergeant George Carter race across weed-choked Dockland to the melancholy sun-flooded ruin of a soot-blackened warehouse, open to the elements, left by time's tide. Beneath an immensity of sky, out of breath, gasping, bent at the waist, beaten, scowling; *'cocky bastard nonce . . .'*

Now, in the late autumn of 1982, there is a sense of a change. Something to do with electronics and digital technology; with new politics, new money, and the consequences, among other things, of a comparatively trivial event such as punk.

Here is the presentiment of a new world rising against an old world, beyond the frozen landscapes and scratchy singles in picture sleeves, and despite the loathing of most punk-era musicians and artists for the new Conservative administration (and most vehemently, for the figure – one might suppose the actual body – of the prime minister herself). Now, beyond the bleak midwinter, something is shifting . . . The bright shops, the quickening city . . .

Back to Marc Almond, therefore, who could have danced to the electro-pop beat on his Walkman through the tube station booking hall, slid down the handrail of the steep escalator, done a neat about-turn and found himself facing the beginnings of an extraordinary work of contemporary art, conceived and commissioned likewise in 1979, but, due to its scale and ambition, a while in the making.

Hitherto, the subways, hallways, stairwells and platforms (and Tottenham Court Road station, where the Northern Line and Central Line converge, seems more labyrinthine than most) had always been dank and bland, Orwellian, faintly threatening, a punk-electro-pop backdrop if ever there was one. Now, these same walls are being gradually covered in a vivid and complex mosaic: in places there are seemingly abstract patterns; elsewhere, objects, people, animals, activities, events are depicted, like futuristic pictograms on the side of a spacecraft.

The tens of thousands of individual tiles — each little bigger than a postage stamp — have a smooth, lustrous glaze that seems to both soften and define their colours. Walking on, you might further imagine that you are exploring an archaeological site of the distant future; as though artist craftspeople of the year 5000 had created a set of richly coloured mosaic murals depicting how they imagined quotidian life in London over three millennia earlier – before an apocalypse, perhaps, that all those industrial-noise bands like S.P.K. and T/G and Rema-Rema had somehow, psychically, picked up on but been unable to prevent.

Designed by the Scottish sculptor and artist Eduardo Paolozzi, and installed between 1982 and 1984, the mosaics at Tottenham Court Road tube station (like those in the entrance hall of the National Gallery, just down the road, where we find in the illustrious throng of British modernist heroes and mystics, Churchill defying the Devil, and Dame Edith Sitwell representing the Sixth Sense) will become curiously overlooked during the next thirty years – their familiarity, perhaps, rendering them invisible.

But in November 1982, the colours are fresh and alive: on the Central Line westbound platform, for example – red, yellow, purple, pink, aqua, leaf green, wood brown, on a silvery, bone-white background; such vivacious colours (reminiscent of the psychedelic animation of The Beatles' third feature film *Yellow Submarine*, made nearly fifteen years earlier) yet here and now resembling primitive pixilation – *patterns beyond Pop* . . .

Abstract panels overlay geometric shapes in dizzying tessellations; then we see saxophones (a nod to the old Soho jazz clubs), a mask, a cross section of a human head, ditto a machine; then a bomber, a bull, a butterfly; a modern man (casual clothes) striding into his day; the totality of the ceramic-pixelated patterning reminiscent once again of an arcade video game, machine-like, vaguely electronic, laboratory-like, modern urban tribal: a premonition of the coming post-Pop, Computer-Caffeine-Commuter Age, when worker citizens will travel wired, dressed in militarised sportswear with their coffee and technology.

As Paolozzi is credited with being one of the pioneers of British Pop art, in the very early 1950s, so here, therefore, he seems to envisage an evolutionary jump, where Pop – its vivaciousness, machine energy, wit and urbanity, its domestic familiarity with trademarks and products and mass culture – becomes something consequent not just on the electrical and the mechanical, but the digital.

His murals share a frequency with Soft Cell's cusp-of-the-computer-era update of 'What' (Pop art styling for post-pop people); with Walkman stereo cassette players (the first headphones widely worn publicly, for personal music on the move); with the burgeoning, almost postmodern Beat Boom revivalism taking off a block away in old Soho; with the new technology gadgets in the flourishing electronics shops on the Tottenham Court Road in 1982 . . .

. . . with the dawn chorus 'style' culture of cool design; *liplicking, unzipping, Harpers and Queens* . . .' sings elegant Martin Fry, that same year, on the epoch-defining, orchestra, funk bass, sleigh bells and Fairlight CMI-boosted album *The Lexicon of Love* by his group ABC – a former Sheffield post-punk reborn in a Billy Fury, Elvis-by-way-of-Birkenhead gold lamé suit; with the video age; with change in the air – the faintly freshening breeze.

Marc Almond, meanwhile, is an artist, like Eduardo Paolozzi is an artist; like all artists he has things to be doing, and a restless energy to live with. He dances on, to ancient concerns such as those engaged by Cocteau and Genet and Lorca, having made the depiction of the new electronic-digital world a more thrilling place with his presence.

And we had all been finding our way to the station.

Subways and platforms, suburban trains and 'Metal Box': first week of January, 1980

White sky, white fog at frozen midday; the white of strip lighting encased in shallow planks of dirty plastic. Seen through train windows, streaked with freezing droplets of melted snow, the evenly spaced trees that grow along the top of the railway embankment look black and squat and muscular and twisted and symbolist – somehow Belgian or Nordic – against the fog and white sky that smell of mud and cold.

In these inner suburbs – Tulse Hill, North Dulwich, along that line – through which the near-empty, tobacco-musty slam-door commuter train makes no effort to hurry, the squat and twisted trees become more ghostly. Palely sinister, yet visually mute, they mark a terrain of mist-hung open spaces in the midst of terraces and villas; the embankment subsumed by unchecked suburban scrub of silver birch, dense weeds, ivy – and the loneliness of empty trains at noon, traversing the empty day.

The soundtrack for this day, however, is repetitive-hypnotic, urgent, scything and metallic guitar, clanking like a pylon strut hit with a torque wrench; juddering fathomless bass, Jamaican inspired; squeaking and spluttering bursts of electronics. And the mad thin male voice – the voice of a self-loathing world-hating Victorian malcontent, bounced through time off a satellite in airless dark – shrieks and whines, intones, insinuates, a roar becoming a retch, at times dully flat, remote, then sneering, letting out a sudden abbreviated scream . . . The sound jumps from upstage to foreground, a sonic acceleration, pulling up to the bumper, from nearly muffled to confrontationally present.

The music is plutonium heavy, each track a length of shorn-off girder, and cold, cold: a post-industrial *Winterreise* ('*Now the world is so bleak, The way shrouded in snow . . .*'), an inner-suburban song of the Earth ('*Life is dark, as is death*'); a vengeful *De Profundis* from a place of abandoned allotments and overhead cables, metal-fenced electricity substations, dripping urban undergrowth, buddleia and brambles, isolated Gothic Revival houses, silently winking control panel lights, spliff pungency, thin raincoats, razor cuts – Lydon to play, grumbling whine; a messenger spirit pinned beneath a waterfall: '*I don't like hiding in this foliage and peat – It's wet, and I'm losing my body heat . . .*'

Andrei Tarkovsky's film of the previous year, *Stalker*, comes to mind; it's like we're in the Zone.

What are the roots that clutch, what branches grow . . . from the memory of a circular metal box, the smooth brushed matt silver of aluminium, such as might once have held a spool of film, and now embossed – with the weirdly elegant brutalism of mass production – with a minimal circular-alphabetic logo: 'PiL'. The metal is thin, like some astro-industrial by-product, and dents easily; soon these metal boxes will seem more machine punched, more pristine in their utter impersonality, for becoming damaged: they wear the scars of indifference and event, their material articulating the passage of time. They look like things that were stored in the future to be exhumed in the past.

Once opened, the box revealed three black vinyl records separated by circular sheets of thin, white, cheap-looking paper; the packaging seemed designed to aggress – conceptually as much as physically – against the product, creating immediate difficulties for the purchaser struggling to enter and possess their mystery: to play them you risk wrecking them.

These records have stark red, white and black labels in their centre, printed on rough paper, and a deep shine; their grooves shimmer as though with the resonance of the near sub-sonic bass they contain, shadowing the whining, intoning, roaring voice and the scattergun electronics and the buzz-saw screaming guitar and the ponderous chords of a string synthesiser.

Foggier yet, and colder! Piercing, searching, biting, cold. Music made of winter. The train and the frozen snow and the twisted black trees, in early January, 1980.

Inside the Night: Knorr, Richon and Willats, late '70s – 1983

Down, down . . . The Roxy and the Vortex.

Swastikas, dusty grey or black jackets, crude eyeliner, plastic surfer-rock sunglasses, a single black leather glove; someone wearing gold Lurex trousers; on white nylon school shirts, handwritten and hand-painted slogans: '1977 YOUR ON THE NEVER NEVER', 'WE AN'T PROUD', 'RIOT', 'SEX PISTOLS'. Girls with short, badly cut hair; boys, ditto. The zombie stare. The dead girl teenage prostitute look; bare young breasts through sheer tops. Safety pins and safety pin chains. Miniskirts and black suspenders. Batwing eyeshadow. The smooth skin of youth. Bash Street Kids.

The aftermath of the overload of the old electric Mass Age, as though from the inside of a dead reactor – such a violent break from all that has gone before and all that is not itself. Games with speed: acceleration and deceleration; fast music that becomes a blur or a dirge; clothes that make it hard to walk, clothes designed to fall apart; music, ditto; sexuality rendered simultaneously hostile and pornographic; a state of sci-fi ruination that is likewise hyper-energised and beyond caring. A fusion of the direct and the oblique.

Glacial-faced residents of Belgravia, a spit from Harrods. Punks and Belgravians: two closed worlds, equally exclusive, equally self-aware.

A portrait within an interior. Ubiquitous Empire style, but cold and godless, shabby, unloved – just owned. Imperious, arrogant, slab-faced, dysfunctional, remote, bewildered, poised – the Belgravian subjects only occasionally make eye contact with the camera; a young man in a double-breasted blazer stands side-on to a low table and a sofa, between two tall windows partially covered by heavily ruched and flounced curtains. *'If the Hostages in Iran are released,'* – runs a caption beneath the image – *'gold will plunge.'*

Another young man: handsome, dark suited and faintly rugged. He pulls a profile, unsmiling; he would slip without effort into Spandau Ballet – the reigning house band of club-culture exclusivity. 'Gold!' they will proclaim in song, heralding an epoch.

Insular, extreme groups, linked by their obsessions with social camouflage, snobbishness, ideological plumage, intolerance and mystique. Rude and chic and clever. The affinity in England between yob and snob is long-standing ('Can a Burchill look at a Churchill?' wrote journalist Julie Burchill, of her own working class relation to the aristocracy) and based in part upon the contempt of both for the middle classes.

But the city beyond these expensive windows remains at this time – '81, '82 – dark and filled with urban mystery; yet to be prised opened up by the new economy, new technology, new consumerism; the Digital Age still, for most people, some way off. We are still in the modernist city; the mechanical city; the service industry city of an electric age of cables and levers and lift gate railings and gunmetal casing and Sony Trinitron.

And the shadows of the 1970s remain, and within one of the darkest, off Villiers Street in Charing Cross, is a club for nocturnal types called The Cha Cha Club. Subject, in 1982, of artworks and documentation by Stephen Willats.

'This work concerned one manifestation of those private clubs: an extreme rejection of society's values, an alienation from its idealisations, that found expression in non-conformity and through the display of aggressively tangential codes of dress and behaviour.'

In *Cha Cha Cha* and later *Doppelgänger* (1985) – images (romantic) and interview statements of urban alienation: nightlife as a parallel reality, tower blocks, desolation and dressing up; young workers (manageress, civil servant, stockbroker) living double lives, their day and night-time selves – Willats showed the slumbering old age of brutalist pre-digital London as an urban theatre; a sub-culture of young people for whom wearing a mask was a need, a job, a work of art and their truth. The one idea for which they could live and die; existential.

A manageress says: '*If anything happens at all it must happen inside, there's absolutely no sign of it happening outside, there's nowhere for anything to happen.*' Bitchy, moody, terminally disaffected. How many packed it in and settled down? As many as died, perhaps. But Wilde vindicated: the truth of masks; a young woman (daytime civil servant, night-time switchblade and leather vamp) says: '*I would state my profession as equally between office worker and actress.*'

Willats's *Living Like a Goya* (1983): mannequin, photos, notes, razor, Anadin and debris;

the half-hidden young woman, recreating herself as a mythic art creature – the portrait of Doña Isabel de Porcel comes to mind, circa 1800 – three nights a week, all black-lace headdress, cleavage and veils; she might have worked in an office somewhere, walking briskly through Holborn each morning, around a quarter to nine.

Blax, Sicilian Avenue, WC1 – dressing like a Vorticist

A sound like ice cracking; a new softness in the air, pushing back the edge of the cold. Hyacinth days. The afternoon light lasts longer; grey-blue streets at 6 p.m.

At Holborn – neither West End nor City, but with something of the mood of both – the diagonal precinct thoroughfare of Sicilian Avenue, in the spring of 1983, clipping a corner of Southampton Row, has its own air of hidden splendour: a flourish of European elegance circa 1910, in this ornate, many-pillared spacious

41

avenue of peach-copper brick bay-windowed mansion flats and turret rooms, rising four storeys above what seem exquisite emporia, or transmissions of same across seven decades.

Through Holborn and the Bloomsbury squares one had time-travelled, Kraftwerk on the Walkman, to what felt like vivid contact with the cities of the old Imperial civilisation of Europe, pre-1914 – *'we stopped in the colonnade, and went on in sunlight . . .'* And with something coming that hates us; but for today, at least, the pink buttonhole, the cinnamon-brown suit, the silk tie flecked pale blue; *'and drank coffee, and talked for an hour . . .'*

In 1910 – Wyndham Lewis meets Ezra Pound at the old Vienna Café; there in the wedge formed by Hart Street and Holborn – and, along with the Café Royale, the only truly continental café in London: '. . . *had the tarnished polish'* (wrote Lewis) *'of the most gilded cafés of five or six continental capitals . . .'*; it's passing later lamented by Pound:

in those days (pre-1914)
  the loss of a café
    meant the end of a B.M. era
    (British Museum era)

The end of an era . . . Milan, Warsaw, Berlin, St Petersburg, Paris, Brussels – *Trans-Europe Express* – already extinct these last seventy years; but we catch their mood like a ribbon of cologne or cigar smoke on the softening breeze; the chamber theatres of their defining service industries – shoe shops and barbers and tobacconists, fancy confectioners, silk scarves and outfitters, department stores, restaurants *deluxe*, grand hotels, ubiquitous dusty fronded palms – still there, or rather, somehow, here, in London WC1, in glimpses, in the early 1980s.

Phantasms of modernism, erratic fragments left by the glacier of time, preserved, ghost shops linger in the modern daylight, and are now best employed as ready-made film sets for the imaginary films being made by and starring – in their heads – young people of a certain disposition . . .

European modernism – its received idea, its reach to New York and the Midwest even – has seemed attuned to the twilit deep midwinter of post-punk, part of that map, and now it's here still in the sense of a spring's earliest gathering, as the span of seven years can be described by four seasons.

Dada, the neoclassical; moss and pine needles, the avenue through the autumnal park; the echoing hallway of a Berlin apartment building, coal heated; electronics, mist and cold; the pretty Viennese mother walks holding her child's hand; young men with side-parted hair wearing silver-grey shirts and blood-red ties, resembling Chicago bank clerks circa 1931. Germany to America; but all of this annexed to stark minimalism and minor chords: melancholy.

'Subway', a stand-out track released this year by the unpleasantly named, NY-based duo Thick Pigeon, caught the mood, precisely. Lulling, hypnotic, gentle repetitive overlayers of electric keyboard notes, a near-electronic fizz on the mid-tones, murmuring like a sunlit stream yet as serially urban as any metro system. A woman's voice, Euro-American, more or less speaking, softly and impersonally, list-like, staccato 'lyrics' – obscure imagism, but as though reported rather than felt; something about boys liking to urinate in corners; then snagging on a memorable phrase, which is repeated to the track's close, changing with each repetition from English to phonetic German, then to just spoken sounds that might be phonetic German: *'The dirt gets in the way; Die - dirt - get - in - der - way. Die durt, get in die-vay; Die dum, dar din der day . . .'*

Drawn to fantasies of elegance and heightened style, their romance sharpened by portent, burgeoning political trauma; a sense of the end of time – the *'Weimardammerung'* come to London. (It seems inevitable that the compound term to describe this complex, expressionist mood would be German, albeit dreamt up by an Englishman (Stephen Spender) visiting Hamburg a half-century earlier.) A transitional pageant that is at once nostalgic and anticipatory – dressing up for the violet hour of an age, as European gentlemen and ladies . . .

Musically, the terrain had been pioneered as early as 1980 by auteur nostalgics for modernism, Les Disques du Crépuscule: a Brussels-based record label whose releases fused modernist melancholy with US/UK post-punk poetics and lilting European new wave easy listening. Aesthetes. Stylists. Black-and-white photographs of classical statuary; a park in Bruges, early evening, snow light . . .

Now, in Holborn, a young man, medium build, his prematurely silvering hair cut short, watered flat, side-parted in a severe line, wearing a cinnamon-brown three-piece suit, cut precisely from a pattern dated 1911 (trimmer, finer, more sleek than one might imagine); gold tie, blue shirt, art deco silver links; cuffed trousers that reach almost to his sternum, pressed from their front pleats to a razor-sharp crease, held taut by broad, elasticised fabric braces of magenta and grey . . . makes his way down Sicilian Avenue, to a small shop, a gentlemen's tailors and outfitters . . .

He carries a silver-topped walking stick; his gloves are of lemon-yellow suede. His shoes, burnished chestnut Oxfords, make a solid and satisfying crunch on the pavement with each brisk step . . . Oh, where have you been, my blue-eyed *sonnenkind*?

In a presentiment of science fiction. His sub-let concrete council flat – circa 1974, the year of the *Diamond Dogs* – looks down on the Space Age silver-cube Faraday memorial on the roundabout at Elephant and Castle; at this time tunnelled by barely lit concrete subways, foreboding after dark, fag smoke, piss and damp, via which one can reach the Bakerloo

Line: the low, dimly yellow-lit carriages, on which our man always thinks, rattling up West, are upholstered in a tufted fabric of medieval colours, that smells of cinders and musty newsprint.

As his gloved hand reaches for the door of the small shop on Sicilian Avenue, his recreation of another time, another place, is complete: setting, costume, event conflate, recreating a notion of the past that is a faintly misregistered but densely stamped impression of another age – the past as a style as another country: as a territory of oneself, as a charade to act out public image and private myth.

His destination – Blax, tailor and outfitters, specialism gentlemen's attire as worn by Edwardians and young men of the Jazz Age – might be seen as an embassy of this particular strand of sub-cultural time-travel. Nothing is missing in Blax, from trench coat to collar stud, rich autumn tweeds, Sunday sunset over Surrey Scots pines and sandy heath; white tie, Oxford bags, City suit. The house models should be Aldous Huxley and Louis MacNeice. The latter wrote:

(Somebody stopped the moving stairs):
Time was away and somewhere else.

Now the wiry male assistant, our man's reflection, has the physiognomy and skin texture of a person from his chosen and reconjured age: a face from the last Imperial twilight – yet likewise related, in style and countenance, to the Beat Boom revivalism, Palladium nights, Cockney patter at the fitting, *'Cost you an arm and a leg . . .'*

Two dandies of the 'The Waste Land' era, time-travelling; one speaks quick, Kingsland Road E1, the other Home Counties; a silver cigarette case, opened to un-tipped Senior Service, is offered; the pale light seems to tint the shop's interior the shade of oyster-coloured gauze – even this afternoon crepuscule seems from a stage further back.

Two friends, whose icy plangent serial phasing guitar and tape loop sound poems are beginning to attract attention, aim to undo such too-easy (in their view) bourgeois acceptance by making their first single – and here's the mad part – by making their first single in the medium *of a sculpture*. A balsa wood glider, one third life-sized, to be exact, that they will display on a Saturday morning in a shopping centre, they say, in some suburban town somewhere, or under a railway arch, out towards the Lea Valley. Title: *Dressing Like A Vorticist*.

A statement to rally around – I.C.A. café, September, 1982

Pale face, dark eyes, crazy hair; twenty-one years old. She sits with bootlaces around her wrists, dressed in black jodhpurs, kung-fu slippers, some old man's shirt and a black leather blazer.

SOUVENIR

She is looking at some photographs by Deborah Turbeville – wintry broken-down European landscapes, tall women in skull-caps, like they've had talcum powder thrown in their faces; derelict chateau rooms and dripping parkland – rococo ball gowns; girl pupils and discipline; wooden struts behind fallen plaster; old wardrobes, classical statues; modern women in cold corridors with sad and remote expressions.

She remembers Joy Division – like watching silvery-black film; guitar, bass and drums like a nail gun in an echo chamber; singer Ian Curtis staring wide-eyed but looking like he was blind; the pale face of a drugged angel, his schoolboy fringe plastered ragged on his clammy sweating forehead; he suddenly danced backwards on his toes, shoulders hunched, hands snatching wildly, arms jerking. His wild-eyed dancing, yes, resembled silvery-black film from 1917 of a shell-shock victim, moving in broken automaton convulsions.

The generation of young intelligentsia who grew up during the years following the Great War of 1914–1918 knew only one document, one single statement, that they could rally around: T.S. Eliot's poem *The Waste Land*; it spoke for them, they felt, even though much of it, or because much of it, seemed almost incomprehensible.

And she sits in a world before computers but towards the dusk of the electrical-mechanical city, aware of Letraset and Xerox art and the power of the drum machine, and phrases like 'malicious glamour', and wonders what her rallying statement might be or have been: *Never Mind the Bollocks*? Andy Warhol's *Interview*, *The Second Sex*, Steve Strange, *Gainsbourg Percussions*?

But it could be so many things, and she looks at the photographs and their desolate romantic world, and thinks only: 'I want to live there.'

SOUVENIR

Exhibition of Polaroid photographs: Ladbroke Grove, September, 1983

The house is typically tall – five storeys, if you include the basement flat, shuttered beneath padlocked area steps – and typically stucco-fronted; also typically for the time, the stucco is peeling and blistered and rotten after years of neglect. Big bay windows on the ground and first floors, the latter opening onto a narrow balcony, deep with soil-like grime, on which stands a small decaying table.

This particular terrace runs downhill – each house with its pillared, dirty chequerboard porch, and two worn steps to the pigeon-grey pavement – and faces a square, surrounded by black railings, into which one cannot see. Tall evergreens, overgrown rhododendrons and azaleas, a vast rosemary bush, brambles, an orange milk crate, rotting newsprint, some cherry trees. In the centre, four or five giant conifers, dusty and greenish black, pungently aromatic, soar into a cloudless blue sky. There is something ecclesiastical about their darkness; their blackness against the pale blue sky reminiscent of a painting by Magritte.

Today, the lulling warmth of an Indian Summer sedates these squares and terraces, which just now are silent, in early afternoon, the slightest sound amplified. The dead heat of London in August had been followed by sudden storms, to be replaced by these soaring blue and gold days, almost hot.

At the house we are visiting – owned by someone's grandparents we think, now shared, or squatted, run-down, rooms emptied of their furniture, stretched swags of black dust against delicate Wedgwood blue in high corners; cracked etched glass in the black-framed door at the end of the long cold hall – the first impression is olfactory; of dense swathes of musky-fragrant silver smoke, rising up from clumps of incense to fold like linen into the slanting sunbeams that fall through rotting sash windows. The incense sticks are stuck in glazed flowerpots of aesthetic blue and white, that also hold dying geraniums, pink and white.

There is an exhibition here, of Polaroid photographs. The photographs show: a young man's torso, striped by the shadows of a Venetian blind; the glow of an ice-blue television screen, surrounded by darkness, on which is a close-up image of a woman's mouth, lips parted, gold glitter lipstick; two boys stripped to the waist stirring a glass tank of blue liquid; a bonfire on a beach against an angry sunset – dark clouds over the sea.

These images accompany, and are accompanied by, a long piece of piano music that is only available on a cassette – that has been compared to the music of Erik Satie, to that of Brian Eno. And anyway, we're here. No one stopped us from coming in; the front door was open.

People are moving to Brussels, to Antwerp, to Berlin. The idea of these cities seems to describe a shift in creative sensibility. '. . . *Die-durt-get-in-die-vay* . . .' People are moving to Chicago; to L.A. An essay in a magazine about sadomasochism and philosophy: that post-structural abjection reflects its desire to disrupt complacencies in a nostalgia for modernism. Illustrations from the graphic novelisation by Guido Crepax of De Sade's *La nouvelle Justine.*

Two evil queens, off duty, but still hostile and malign, are on the first floor, loftily perambulating the empty rooms (the silver high heels of one echoing on the bare boards); shoulder bags, plastic trousers, ivory white cotton pantaloons, cheesecloth shirt knotted just beneath the sternum, blue PVC biker jacket, drawn-in eyebrows, blusher, cheek-bones like wing-mirrors, hair full of rags and ribbons, Breton fisherman's cap . . . They glance towards us with expressions that barb indifference with contempt. This accomplished, they wander into the adjoining room.

There had been a supper party in a second-floor flat, just off Mortimer Street; a narrow street, in shadow; another hot evening, airless, earlier that summer; the windows were open to a view of the red brick bulk of the eastern wall of Middlesex Hospital. Acrid musty herbal tea; some kind of consommé made of dissolving dried fish. Where was a Department of Toxicology? (it was asked), prompting brief discussion of poisons and their effectiveness, and of a homosexual brothel that used to be close by, or next door, purportedly established by or for the Duke of Clarence, frequented by The Ripper. Sodomy, rape, murder.

Then suddenly, child-like: 'Mm – jelly! My favourite!'

A youngish male dealer in surrealist literature, carefully pouring tea, with utmost deferential courtesy, solicitously bending forward, finger on cast-iron teapot lid, long lank fringe hanging over his face, the grey fabric of his suit jacket strangely stiff. Wearing the mask of the shy bachelor connoisseur, obedient to archaic bourgeois niceties; a female Japanese film-maker – friendly, charismatic, abrupt: heavy grey skirt, black knee-socks, black hair cut and dyed into a tangerine orange pom-pom on the back of her head; she speaks of clockwork dinosaurs re-enacting *Double Indemnity*.

An emaciated German dressed in black. He has said – in all seriousness – that he is a student of the Tibetan thigh-bone trumpet. Magical music that can affect the course of events – music aimed as much as played. In a band, in a commune in Kreuzberg; Kurt Schwitters; industrial Dada; runic tattoos; fuck the police.

A Polaroid photograph of pale pink poppies in a blue garden; description by an older, flamboyantly effeminate man of how a corpse sits up during the process of cremation.

Like trying to move and speak in dense and heavy air; no trance of sensuous, free or easy movement, neither fluidity nor youth. Were they forbidden alcohol (there was none) or did they share some condition that meant their systems would not tolerate wine?

And did we meet the Devil thus? For their enthusiasms seemed focused, wholly, on *expérience limite*, madness, violent death, catastrophe; the intellectualising, through histories of psychology, literature and critical theory, and threading through sub-culture, of extreme acts, rituals, so-called 'transgression' – any taboo would do, it seemed. A reprise of the melodramatic horrors that had so excited the French Decadents a century before; only sourer, routed through an industrial-occult aesthetic . . .

Clever, in some ways; intellectually cunning, attractive when they wanted. These denizens of a dark fold in the city's fabric were above all perilous to the weakened, lost or self-doubting;

any of whom, and with immense charm — the men suddenly fraternal, smilingly affectionate, the women encouraging, laughing, almost flirtatious — they might attempt to recruit to their airless, drear and ultimately doomed philosophy.

All of this had led somehow to the house in Notting Hill, and now we stood in the ruins — empty, elegiac, bearing a deep imprint of time and event — of an earlier revolution still; the tall house, while playing host to the present, filled with the clamouring echo of that revolt, an angry silence — the fitting context for a particular lineage: performance art as ritual, knowledge to be found on the edge of experience; the body as the site for the gaining of that knowledge.

These Polaroid photographs, by contrast, were deeply English, neo-Romantic in spirit: Paul Nash, John Minton, Derek Jarman; the lane in deep green evening light, abstraction on the beach, the personality of inanimate objects (a jar on a windowsill, a dirty windowpane, a stricken tree, moss on blackened brick); the stilled or violent atmosphere of time and place thickening to numinosity.

Rags and ribbons in the hair; blue PVC; young men in heavy make-up; distant piano music; the longest river in the world – as though into the twisting interior of a tall, rotting house and the past.

The older Revolution, an earlier London

1971, '72. So many they had known had shared the path into exile. The countercultural diaspora of King's Cross and Hackney, Brixton, Camden Town and Notting Hill Gate.

And there had been more than a nuance of fantasy in the way that this couple – she with a dirty blue quilted anorak over her long dress of crimson crushed velvet, her brown ringlets falling loosely between her shoulder blades – had left their old flat in the Caledonian Road, in the cold early spring of 1971, and headed north to remote coastal country: a damp, half-ruined cottage and a new life.

At the time, it had seemed, from the squats and polytechnics, the art schools and communes, a whole urban tribe had quit the capital; setting off to pit villages tucked into some furrow of moorland, or to the chilly, high-ceilinged Victorian terraces of provincial university cities; to crofts and to smallhold-ings where the black ditches ran with ice water for half of the year. There, the fortu-nate ones raised families, became teachers, gardeners, homeopaths, social workers; while others fell through the cracks between an old life and a new; became recluses, eccentrics, *'nowhere to go but indoors . . .'*, junkies, small-town alcoholics . . .

Once they had been looking for peace and love and freedom – that was the idea: planning revolt, planning Eden – against which they believed a new age of concrete and plastic and fascist war and money was ranging its brute aggression.

. . . the seminar room at Essex in the late '60s – first year American Studies: rain beating against the narrow windows as the lights were being turned on. Back in those days, twisty-faced Edgar Allan Poe had been in the pantheon: freeing his mind, going in to get out. But now – now the drear landscape bares its teeth.

It had seemed inconceivable to leave London, however run-down the city, or compromised the cause. For London had been the complex network and arcane administration of a mindset: events, experiments, statements, infrastructure, celebrations, discourse and protest. A follower of fashion comes suddenly and vividly to mind: a brisk, slender figure, crossing the road in bright sunshine, Earl's Court – his shoulders thin and tensed inside a putty-coloured raincoat, a cigarette hanging from the corner of his mouth; yet so self-assured, elegant . . .

In the old system of social categories, such a character had been urban, not ruralist, nor retreating to the cult of the child; full of iconoclasm, rather – Baudelaire, Huxley and Sartre. While others had been dedicated to Nature, and to the Revolution, and to all that seemed real, politically, as to a god.

As to a god . . . '*Well, you know, we all want to change the world*' – so mockingly cool, that reproach from on high.

Red brick mansion flats – their outline grey in a pale mist, suffused by the white gold light of a low winter sun; wet pavements, old shop fronts and pub doorways, their paintwork peeling – an ancient time of groceries wrapped in newspaper: spuds, beans, tins of sardines and rice pudding; joints and Cornflakes.

Thick hair, through which clear brown eyes, like those of young children, seemed to stare both vacant and helpless from pale expressionless faces. Heavy greatcoats, damp, reeking of syrupy patchouli; tarnished military buttons, unwashed jeans and black suede ankle boots; mornings of fog and fine rain – the Cromwell Road a drab vista of dingy mansions, some of their high windows with rags and flags for curtains . . .

And endless, endlessly strange rooms – rooms painted black, rooms thick with the muscular reek of pot; rooms papered with posters – Frank Zappa, Che, topless black girl astride a motorbike, Steve McQueen, Import Cargo, St Louis, circa 1911; rooms that opened off other rooms down corridors which had once led to servants' rooms and sculleries – now illuminated by dim red light bulbs and rank with mildew, the unchecked foliage of the overgrown garden pushing against the windows as though to overrun the house; sunlit rooms haunted by a broken promise of benign domesticity – placid long-haired couples baking bread, restoring Eden in Paddington or Maida Vale . . .

Yet all had been transient, and, ultimately, illusory: mere mirages in a vast expanse of squatted and rented accommodation, where nothing was ever as it seemed and the only logic to be celebrated was a switchback of contradictions and reversed affirmatives. When anyone, for example, had asked a straight question, you might reply, 'Yes No' or 'No Yes' or 'Dada'. To reverse language and action had been a favourite reflex – a necromantic device, hippy curse to Stick It to the Man.

Of course, your interlocutors could never know and were not meant to know. To be as slippery as spilt mercury was the aim, and then to reverse the scatter of soft hard particles into a single mass once more. To run alongside the windows of the bus and hold a mirror up to the visiting tourists, as they leaned out with their cameras . . .

And then, history would record: '. . . *after all the sound and the fury, it was over and silence returned. One by one the rebel causes swiftly fell. The student anger seemed to have burnt itself out; the protests stopped. There were no more sit-ins, no more excited votes, and no more invasions . . .*'

A pause between the old Revolution and the local riots of '76. These big old houses, busted up into bedsits; fast drugs and concrete; graffiti on the underpass; the loneliness of violet street lights against the evening sky. Cold October wind through the sash windows, left open for days on end; rain blowing in, puddles by the rug. West Indians, theatricals, those pursuing an art-directed lifestyle; your first gay sound system; *42nd Street* projected on the wall at a party; Jagger eternal, stroppy Mod vision of Deep South: '. . . *gimme little drink, from your loving cup . . .*'

Time passed. So many Saturday nights, so many bright mornings of sharp frost and wet weekday evenings; traffic, weddings, gales in autumn, breast cancer; Sunday papers, scaffolding heights; London updated. 1983.

Su Tissue, Suburban Lawns and Salon de Musique

Nearly a century before, visiting Omaha, Oscar Wilde had remarked, 'If ever America produces a great musician, let him write a machinery symphony.'

And racing a century forward, from southern California, a group called Suburban Lawns are a local cult. Spiky art school frenetic guitar-driven scales and repetitions, drumbeat marking time, sudden dead stops mid-track; shades of jazz fusion amid basic surf-pop-punk-rock *povera*.

Vocalist and co-lyricist is Su Tissue, whom pundits of the time – with a mix of reverence and cynicism – say resembles a fourteen-year-old Sunday School assistant.

Waist-length black hair, dark eyebrows, a library card Pocahontas of seemingly formidable self-possession and reserve – her voice low, velvety, aching, at times almost Germanic; then mad, like a helium squeak from the throat of Yoko Ono. As though Dusty Springfield had tutored with Devo.

Voluptuous mouth, her hazel eyes always avoiding eye contact, aloof, disturbing, disdainful. The mad girl at a party – frightening energy that warns off the attracted; yet the collision between her on-stage persona – unsmiling conservative elusive – and her unselfconscious vocal extremism is instantly compelling.

Some meagre film footage records them. The all-male band – jeans and T-shirts – dudes, but likewise unsmiling, intent, cool, occasionally energised in an angular manner. Su seeming almost out-of-patience with having to sing, and dressed as though by a strict parent. Lyrics contain words such as 'irrelative' and 'anti-matter' – 'science nerd stuff', the guitarist will later remark – but are enlivened by the deliberate inclusion of misheard phrases: 'I'm a janitor', for example, becoming 'Oh my genitals'. Lyrics made memorable by found mishearings.

'Baby', 'Janitor', 'Gidget Goes To Hell' – an eponymously titled album in 1981 – then they're gone. Su attends Berklee College of Music, recording an album of piano and free-form vocalising, *Salon de Musique*, in 1982, which sounds as though it might have been made by Wim Mertens and/or Steve Reich (repetitions and layers of piano arpeggios – concert grand, a US mid-twentieth century sunlit hall, floor-to-ceiling windows; vocal impressionism, punctuated by taut threads of high electric guitar notes; the whole cumulative, building, sustaining and soaring) yet remains somehow her own, in temper and tone: the mad girl at the party, up before dawn to astonish us all.

Salon de Musique exemplified the dialogue, seldom discussed but increasingly apparent, in certain circles, between early and late modernism. Music and sub-culture for the twilight, the closing scene of that accelerated cultural epoch, which had run now for the best part of a century, driven by the dictate (from Ezra Pound), 'Make It New!'

And so a short step from Suburban Lawns as sophisticated, aggressively modern, art-punk hauteur (they called their own small record label 'Suburban Industrial') to classical-Euro-American modernism; musically: the enfolding articulation of time and time's passing, an urban sublime; linear modernism as a phasing continuum, having almost reached its extent, now folding into something new, beyond modernity: *'Towards the evening of a gone world, the light of its last summer pouring into a Chelsea street . . .'*

Yet somehow, also, so reminiscent of spring; sharing that compelling note, both stilled and tense, that is simultaneously anticipation and nostalgia.

Wembley, the Empire Pool

Remembering 18 March 1972 – it feels like the middle of Pop's Imperial Age. And now a Saturday; late afternoon, suddenly mild after weeks of cold; a featureless expanse of concrete and asphalt. A teenage girl turns quickly to glance in our direction, then turns away again, just as fast. Her face is pale and slightly rounded; in her dark brown hair she wears a plastic grip with a silver star at one end.

The sky is palest blue over suburban north London and too boring to look at for long. Not that anyone here would want to, given the building excitement of this long-awaited occasion, the sense of a gathering, of energy massing: a mass celebration. Something is afoot in this drear landscape of main roads and big gloomy boozers and such an immensity of too-empty sky, pressing depressingly down. Something to oppose, in fact, the despotism – the tyranny of banality – of an afternoon of blank bland skies above the London Borough of Brent.

A motorbike glides by, bringing new arrivals: ape-hanger bars and hardtail stepped seat, extended forks, fat back tyre; its almost idling engine guns like a Spitfire on take-off. It carries two young men in denim and leathers, lumpy-haired UK Easy Riders letting their freak flag fly – no crash helmet required in 1972; they stare coolly ahead, expressions set.

Then more girls: black satin blazers, silver glitter on high teenage cheekbones, Boots 17, shoulder-length flat-looking straight hair, centre partings, bubble perms, tank tops, loon pants, flares and cheesecloth. Nobody has chic or finesse; clothes look simple, crude.

Urgent, restless men in brown suits – somewhere off the timeline between spivs and *The Sweeney* – selling knock-off posters . . .

And yet more girls, and some boys (a few in

dark glasses), taunting the Cockney old soldier commissionaires. The girls look heavier and the boys look skinnier. A chauffeur-driven black Daimler Princess, at this time hire car of choice for celebrities, comes briefly into view – empty but significant. We're at Wembley, the Empire Pool, with solid-gold-super-cosmic tickets to see the biggest pop sensation around: psychedelic bedsit troubadours turned thrillingly and massively electric . . .

Just under four hours pass as the gathering builds to a frenzy: and American DJ and BBC Radio One star 'Emperor' Rosko (then, in Pop's Imperial Age, commanding regular audiences of ten to twenty million listeners) is on stage, working the crowd, brewing the gale of screams: 'Are you ready over there?' he demands, arms outstretched, index fingers pointing; to be answered by a loyal roar, the crowd loving every minute, the build-up . . . 'Are you ready down there?' he asks the front stalls – and they are; everyone on their feet, ecstatic, stares fixed on the stage, eyes shining, entranced – and the equipment on the stage looks so primitive: some 'Orange' trademark amps, a lot of black gaffer tape, a pair of congas stage left, the kind of drum kit you'd expect to find in a room above a pub . . .

But the side stage curtain has twitched in the dimmed house lights, and the gale of screams is deafening as Emperor Rosko announces that just back from their coast-to-coast American tour, for the first time back in the UK, are the one and only, the almighty . . . T. REX . . . Three long-haired young men stride out on to the stage, into the cavernous cathedral of screams . . . George Harrison, an early pioneer of this experience, would later observe that while pop stars may get the money and the applause and the screams, they give the audience their nervous system in return.

And this may be why the three young players have fixed, almost stern expressions

– no wave to the crowd: not a smile in sight. Which also renders them cooler; intent technicians, ready to create a magic so emotionally intense, seeking out every muscle, neurotransmitter, tear, fantasy, pleasure zone, existential core and love impulse in the ten thousand souls who have gathered to watch. Although 'watch' is too simple a verb for an activity which in many – most – cases passes way beyond observation, intellect, reason and objectivity . . .

On bongos, congas, maracas and whistle, Mickey Finn; bass, Steve Currie; drums, Bill Legend . . . A tense acoustic void for a few seconds, in which every sound – every electrical bump, thud and buzz – is massively amplified as the musicians take their places, plug in, check instruments, to a broadside of screams that suddenly attains the seemingly impossible by doubling, at least, in volume, as former ace Mod face, Marc Bolan – now dressed in green satin trousers, metallic silver blazer, guitar slung over his right shoulder, little girlish white Alice shoes with low heel and cross bar, and a T-shirt bearing a drawing of his own mythic face – finally appears on stage with a jauntiness that suggests he would never, of course, keep anyone waiting . . . He shouts 'Yeah!' into the microphone by way of greeting, then shouts 'monitors' to an unseen roadie, before flicking out a brace of choppy chords – sharp, hard, elegant, deafening . . .

And suddenly they're off – powering out the introduction to 'Cadillac' with an energy which lifts the whole occasion far away from glitter-pop fad and into another realm altogether; somewhere not far from black America in spirit – the genesis and arche-typical essence of this rock and roll music form that has been dominating the public imagination, establishing its empire of signs, seemingly unstoppable . . .

Then the band are into a revved-up version of 'Jeepster' (such a gloriously meaningless and instantly pure pop title) from their *Electric Warrior* album. The song should be nearing its end, a switchback of reversing chords, each rise and descent hammered home by three heavier beats. Marc has played the pay-off line to perfection: *'I said, girl I'm just a vampire for your love . . .'* he croons, sliding down the insinuation of the lyric with a throaty drawl, before turning a billion pheromones to fizzy starshine with the knock-out blow: *'And I'm gonna suck ya!!!!'*

He chops out three more chords, taking the track deeper into a rocked-out instrumental – a rocking-rolling-roller-coaster of Bolan boogie, tight, heavy, urgent and deft – and then duck hops along the front of the stage with a swagger not seen since Chuck Berry wowed the crowd with 'Sweet Little Sixteen'; music and musicians are in full, controlled acrobatic flight, utterly assured, finding every nerve . . . a machine in perfect perpetual motion. And when they close, Bolan executes a perfectly timed jump with both feet off the stage, landing on the down chord – it's flawless . . .

But there is more to come; allowing the applause to build, and build, and build, and then begin to dip, Marc saunters casually back to the microphone, as coolly and unconcerned as though he had just wandered into the kitchen, and enquires of the hysterical, pleading audience, still screaming, hands on heads, his for the taking, 'You alright?'

The old Mod cockiness, and that's all the talking done. Such insouciant cool; a world brought to life in the flip of a hand . . .

'*My time is up, I will no longer play-for-you* . . .' announced Sparky's Magic Piano in the eponymous children's story. Could pop stop? Might rock music, as a form and an emblem, as an epoch, become quaint? Impossible to imagine, in March, 1972.

But a case might soon be argued, one way or the other, from Soho, Tyneside or Barlow Moor Road, to the sun-bleached lawns of

Hollywood Forever.

We fade to grey.

Other people read obituaries

It had been written that there is something of Bouvard and Pécuchet – Gustave Flaubert's characters: two seekers-after-truth from modest clerical backgrounds, their boundless enthusiasm for knowledge matched only by the constancy with which it eludes them – about lovers embarked on their first heroic phase.

And so there was something of Bouvard and Pécuchet about the two old-young flâneurs, walking as though bound to the London streets, correlating the walked text and the written text, awkward, out of step with revolt and conformity alike, always searching for something that didn't exist anymore.

Other people read obituaries; they passed comment on the deaths of places they knew:

sudden disappearances, as though lifelong friends and acquaintances had slipped away in deep midwinter, at night. So now they patrolled absences, but still looked, still searched.

Near Euston they met a friend from the old days of punk; memories: The Windsor Castle, Harrow Road, telephone boxes, school pullover, ripped, the National Front, beer smell and feedback.

He said, 'I cannot stand this reign of shit. And I think I've cracked a rib.'

Sunset

The bedroom is painted silvery-white, which at dusk, in half light, bamboo roller blind half lowered, can appear faintly marbled or mottled moss green – which makes the whiteness colder, the room more still. Ceiling, walls, picture rail, skirting boards and wooden mantelpiece: all silvery, greenish white.

Oh, what a universe is here!

On the mantelpiece, a narrow vase of violet-blue glass holds two stems of heavily perfumed freesia – the flowers bright yellow and flame. In summer, at sunset, a stretched oblong of amber light falls on the room's one picture, a poster of Wallis's *Chatterton* – '*and burned is Apollo's laurel bough*' – the teenage poet suicide, alabaster in death, head turned, his long hair the same colour flame as the freesias to one side, which appear increasingly votive . . .

An office clerk who strove to be a poet! A fantasist scorned as a forger.

After a little while, intensifying tape loop drones laced with arcing feedback build in mesmerising layers, shimmering like the surface of a lake at sunset, at the lighting of the evening star. An innervated, perfumed, suburban dreamworld.

Like many of its neighbours, the house had received enemy fire during World War Two, in the form of incendiary bullets; across the bay of the French windows you can still see a neat, diagonal row of scorch marks in the parquet. In time they have become as much a feature of the room as the inherited piano stool, the oval gilt-framed mirror and the crystal cockerel.

This is London's southern commuter belt; a landscape created in the 1920s across the rural gentility of Edwardian estates, common fields and Victorian cottages. A land, once noted by E.M. Forster, 'of amenities, where success was indistinguishable from failure'.

But that seems harsh. By the time this part of the story ends, early 1980s, the house and its suburban road – mellowed by fifty years of soft April evenings and russet autumn Sundays – still appear a place of unbroken respectability: of order and routine, held fast by codes so rigid that they barely need a name. An outpost of *The Waste Land*? Perhaps; but only in those threadbare places where an old underlying sadness shows through the neatness and modest prosperity – more of a desperate tiredness, perhaps.

And hither we come, to seek the spring.

A low Swedish coffee table, oval, polished light brown wood; sizeable enough to fill a corner; on which books, including – published in 1977 (and adopted as a suburban punk manual) – Martin Green's *Children of the Sun: A Narrative of Decadence in England After 1918*.

The writings and stances, audacities, scandals and acceleration of modernism have seemed to echo in what felt like modernity exhaustion and collapse, as the twentieth century approached its ninth decade; of pop kids as Pierrot, pallid and slender, beseeching fate, taking their place, made-up, in Eliot's *Waste Land*; revisiting the fractured compulsive mood of Giraud's *Pierrot lunaire*, set to music by Schoenberg in 1912: *'The "sprech-gesang" he devised for them later familiar to all Europe as the appropriate music for modern urban melancholy, because it was used for Kurt Weill's operas . . .'*

The years of post-punk's restless influence had indeed reprised – as you listened to the shimmering layers of sound, full of sunset – some early modernist motifs. Punk rock – such a comparatively trivial event . . . But just now, as the smoke was clearing, a new avant-garde: cultish, audacious and declamatory – Make It New! – *l'art pour l'art*, workers versus Tories; semantic games, style as myth-of-oneself, charade, mask and alibi; a platform for transgressive rituals, the industrial-occult, the abject; one night only live at Dresden power station . . .

Greater London, '76–'83; finding ways to the station: one might determine to make any journey – suffer any amount of risk and abuse – to track down the urgent elemental moment contained in the temper of a voice or an electronic sound; a voice and a sound making vivid and so necessary some particular arrangement of mood and words, so modern and clever, admirable, to be followed – from outside common experience; an aura that seemed from a stage further ahead, from a moment of being – minting newness like a new love.

Bedroom dreams; the shimmering layers and arcs and drones; the deepening amber light; sunset; the soft rich scent of freesia as the quiet suburban roads become the colour of blue ash. On the outside was a condition – a state of being; but, yearning for a centre across nine miles of residential housing, dual carriageways, commuter lines, recreation grounds and drab parades of shops, attraction became need, and need the acid bath to strip apathy away, keeping a keen edge on consciousness – too alert, almost, to what could seem like the beginnings of a fantastical spring.

Two

University Bookshop, Gower Street, WC1,
1983

We stopped in Gordon Square and went on in sunlight.

One afternoon, like a premonition – those first few days of the season's change: '. . . *neither sad nor cheerful;*' (writes André Gide, in *The Immoralist*) '*the air here fills one with a kind of vague excitement and induces a state as far removed from cheerfulness as it is from sorrow; perhaps it is happiness.*'

This new mood – it seemed an 'ecstatic melancholy' – was also and not unpleasantly vertiginous; as though many directions had become available simultaneously, after years of no choice at all.

One route took us to Gower Street, Bloomsbury – thoroughfare of London University – and to books, of course, and writing. *'The rich man is speaking to us from his gondola . . .'* The old University Bookshop has an ornate collegiate façade: fussily Gothic windows – imposing, scholastic, bringing to mind the rush and bustle of wet London weekday afternoons, fresh and mild, and high-mindedness and irritating fine-mindedness.

Four floors, ascended by a narrowing staircase – looking for a guide upon the shelves, a manual to this dizzying spring that will explain the association between the present age and the search for a way ahead; at a time when the signposts seem to show the same destination in all directions, collapsing meaning while concentrating atmosphere, portent.

But still it is exciting, this sea of possibilities. The exchange of the era of post-industrial

Winterreise for a time of serious play –
Romantic irony regained; all styles served
here; a carnival *l'heure bleue*, as distances
become harder to gauge.

A literary time, yes; high up overlooking
Gordon Square; an age of books and of
writing.

*'Out of love for mankind, and out of despair
at my embarrassing situation, seeing that I
had accomplished nothing and unable to make
anything easier than it had already been made,
and moved by a genuine interest in those who
make everything easy, I conceived it as my task
to create difficulties everywhere . . .'*

Postmodern pop and ecstatic melancholy

This intimation of a vivid new mood comes
through a fresh pop direction, sometime around
1982, '83.

Less stark and elegiac; looser, from the
heart, seeking the spring, less dragging the

dank heavy seaweed of punk . . . the new mood unfolds, lush and young and sad; a territory defined by the boyish, charming, clever, urgent, obscure, ardently heartfelt debut release in 1982 by Prefab Sprout (the group's strange name a further example of creative mishearing, it transpired – this time of a phrase in Lee Hazlewood and Nancy Sinatra's recording of 'Jackson').

The title of Prefab Sprout's first single – 'Lions In My Own Garden (Exit Someone)' – is imbued with such (intentional or otherwise) seemingly postmodern intermixing of ideas and images and points of view that the erratic-but-cool parenthesis at its end seemed to herald an epoch; in a manner in tune with that of the burgundy songbird on the spout of the Alessi kettle, or the lifts on the outside of the new Lloyd's Building.

Paddy McAloon, the song's author and singer, subsequently revealed that the song's title was an acronym for Limoges – the town where his girlfriend of the time was staying. This felt like an Umberto Eco-style game with narrative and meaning; but it seemed more effective, as regards the interesting ungainliness of the phrase as a title for a pop single, for the listener not to know this biographical footnote.

As a statement – dreaming on – the awkwardly paced yet evocative title seemed also reminiscent of surrealism (to a post-modern novelist or film-maker – Peter Greenaway, for example – mightn't someone such as Leonora Carrington, for example, have observed – on a mild afternoon in late April – lions in her own garden (Lancashire country-side, Mexico City) and the exit of someone?); while at the same time, heard quickly, it seemed to abut a child-like, storybook quality with a stark update of whatever modern might be. Odd, but poetic; figurative yet fantastical; whimsical, complex.

But what did you actually get? The two minutes and thirty-one seconds of the track opened with what sounded like harmonica and xylophone, wistful and melodic, picking up an electric guitar's sharp strumming that gently swung into an easy rock rhythm; a discreet yet rigid drumbeat keeping pace. Punk has fallen away, like the casing of a rocket propulsion system, becoming space debris; but there remains an energy, a compressed intent that even the track's light touches of easy listening do nothing to dilute.

And so the song begins to strengthen with barely concealed muscle.

Enter the male singer's voice – clear, strong, soft Geordie-Irish sharpened with Americana, mellifluous. Above all, this young man's voice is distinct, controlled (but like it has a lot to control), passionate, and exhales youth: *'But I've got this friend who thinks he's in love with you . . .'* (forceful, almost shouted); then, in a rush: *'And it doesn't sum it up to say he's singing the blues . . .'* (the cherry in blossom, the listener might think, as the pacing lion stops and turns to stare, unmoved); and then clever: *'So you're living in Eden, where apples are good . . .'* And the harmonica comes back in, ghost-like, with spaghetti western eeriness, the desert wind and the distant locomotive . . . *'the rumours have started that we are both young . . .'* – harmonica – *'lions in my own garden (exit someone) . . .'* The 'own' in the sentence, when sung, being the little sensation, a minor but distinct awkwardness, that makes it memorable – makes it work.

Here was a memorable mix of the seemingly simple and seemingly complicated, and within the disjunction of these two seemingly seeming positions, a fable seemed to open up, seasonally removed in mood from the sonorous winter-bound elegies of early New Order, or Soft Cell's rain-slicked seedy city, and closer to an ecstatic melancholy attendant on the vagaries of young love.

Music made of winter replaced by music made of violet springtime.

Everything was at once intimated and precise, blending to create an impassioned love song that was about both getting and losing, and which the word 'vernal' might have been invented to describe. You might imagine an Edwardian villa, in some once prosperous provincial suburb, the garden overhung with blue light in the green fragrant evening, heavy white lilac . . . And the pacing lion becoming the someone whom someone else realises they love but might never attain. Sadness and happiness become one, infinitely transferable, stilling the giddy centre of thought.

And all of this . . . romance . . . conveyed not figuratively, in straight narrative and images, but more through a form of post-modern imagism – an assemblage of intim-ations, even overt declamations, that were culturally poetic, emotionally and semantically misregistered, delivered from a particular yet fragmented authorial position. A reasonably traditional pop musical convention (guitar, drums, bass, harmonica, vocals) carrying a strange, fractured, cool, sort-of Cubist idea of a love song, full of longing and loss . . .

The vinyl single sleeve featured a *Vogue* portrait of Edie Sedgwick (necessarily almost) in her Ann-Margret style black tights and pale singlet, lithe arms outstretched like wings, balancing in ballet pose – young, androgynous, embodying Old American graciousness and the erotic . . . Pop-hip, gorgeous, doomed.

Unsurprisingly perhaps, the group's debut album, released in 1984, would be perfectly titled: *Swoon.*

'The Place of Dead Roads', Marylebone, 1983

The statuette was the first thing she noticed – it appeared to dominate the white, low-ceilinged room, with its single wide window looking out on to a backyard that was empty, save for a dwarf cherry tree in full and luminous pink blossom. The light inside the room was like the light that reflects off snow; immediately on entering, one inhaled the cool scent of roses and the warm smell of Virginia tobacco. There was a sharp and potent sense of antiquity.

The little golden Buddha was seated upon the coils of a seven-headed serpent that reared up to protect him from a terrible storm. As a sculptural form it is perfect, this *Mucalinda* – and the example standing on the cheap black Moroccan table was extremely old. Here too was a triumph of reality over appearance: for the statuette appeared savage and frightening, yet tells of the Buddha's protection from the elements, and the joy of the Serpent King who protected him.

And so, at first, she didn't even recognise Bill. She had been expecting, she supposed, some kind of junkie hobo bum; but standing by the fireplace, his hair watered down flat, and wearing a white shirt with double cuffs and antique links, a dark blue silk tie and an immaculate black three-piece suit, was a pinch-faced, severe-looking gentleman of clearly patrician breeding. He had two fingers of his left hand hooked into his waistcoat pocket, and in his right he held a cigarette at chest height. He was staring directly ahead, but unseeing, elsewhere, with those glassy, death's-head eyes.

What kind of reception this was meant to be, she had no idea. But she remembered the heartening, secure feeling of being accepted and belonging, as the host thrust a glass of very cold white wine into her hand. The alcohol hit almost immediately, making everything seem meaningful and admirable and amiable. Her friends seemed at ease with the other people in the room, and were clearly known to some of them.

The host, his head inclined, muttered something to Bill, speaking with a low rumble of laughter; Bill just looked at the floor and made a non-committal sound of agreement, for all the world as though he and his interlocutor were two old college men, sagaciously acknowledging the decline of a noble game.

Only later did she hear Burroughs in action, over dinner.

He was seated at the head of the table. He seldom looked up from his soup, and when he did it was to stare in silence, or to mumble a word to the Hispanic-looking boy at his side. On the table beside him were a pack of Senior Service unfiltered cigarettes and a lighter. Across the table was a flamboyant young gay man – whose name she never did catch. He seemed from the upper classes.

He spoke in an insistent, preening whine and with a frequent nervous, whinnying laugh. Was he stupid or just ill at ease? Rolling his eyes, pouting and stammering as though for punctuation, he frequently made to affirm his sincerity by pressing his palm against his sternum while casting a glance to the ceiling. His sole topic of conversation was the merits and pleasures of being a male homosexual; but most of all, it seemed he wanted Burroughs to join with him in these vocal celebrations of same-sex desire. Drunk, he became too familiar.

'Oh, but William,' he screeched in mock reproach. 'Surely you know the masterpieces of Caravaggio – those gorgeous boys?'

Burroughs, unmoved – and seemingly unaware that he was even being addressed – continued to concentrate upon his consommé.

'I adore the paintings of Caravaggio . . .' the enthusiast continued, undeterred. 'Rape, murder – *it's just a shot away* . . .' And then the whinnying laugh again.

At this, Burroughs laid down his soup spoon and dabbed the corners of his dry, lizard mouth with the corner of his snow-white napkin. There was a beat of silence, during which the entire table turned to face the great man . . .

Then, in the slow, canny, rural drawl of a screwball professor and with the intonation of W.C. Fields, he stated as plain fact: 'Sure – I knew Caravaggio. He was a drag queen in Tangiers

. . .' Another pause. 'But Joe Caravaggio never picked up a brush in his life . . .'

Suddenly seeming like a gathering of animals, the guests all roared with laughter – the voluble art lover loudest of all. You could see them swinging their tails and clacking their hooves as they cackled and hooted.

A chorus of beasts – only Burroughs remained human, in form and appearance at least; but he was translucent, millennia old, absorbed in the passing of aeons and the exchange of one wearisome ceremony for the next.

Queerness

There were some gay men who vehemently resented the disclosure, throughout the AIDS-plagued 1980s, of the older, secret queer world that they remembered. (At the gentlemen's public convenience at London Bridge station, Gilbert & George recalled, a sympathetic attendant would dust the lavatory seat for sixpence.)

Dim lights, white engineering brick, astringent chemical odour, high grilles, black dust, echoing cubicles; darkness, raincoat and briefcase.

It was as though the thrill and mystery, apartness and danger – the criminality, even – which had comprised the glamour of that private realm would evaporate on being revealed, to disappear entirely; like ancient frescoes, long hidden, bright and intact in time-sealed rooms, suddenly exposed to modern air; the pigment to vanish like wind across a dune, in the time it takes to sigh.

Queer memoir seemed the best literature of modern London.

Later, in Manhattan, at icy midwinter sunset, orange sky and freezing iron black, resident alien Quentin Crisp – of Sutton, Surrey – would fulminate against the new liberalism.

'This nonsense,' he spat, 'of soldiers saying they would kill "if they had no other option" . . . They should *long* to kill . . .'

'Violent Silence' – Bloomsbury Theatre, WC1, September, 1984

From late-summer London, rippling pale gold light as if painted by Sickert, into musty dust-black urban darkness. French literature; talking ideas. A celebration of the work of Georges Bataille.

An ideological event, consecrated to shock; confrontation and ritual; radical or just isolated; of choice unconnected to the institutional worlds of contemporary art and literature; derived rather from a periodic table of shared influences and inspirations, which might comprise an index of blasphemers – in the sense of spitters into life's face, including: surrealist pornographers, De Sade, Burroughs, Ballard, Bowles, Duchamp, Genet, Gurdjieff,

SOUVENIR

Crowley, R.D. Laing, Blanchot, Gysin, Giorno
. . .

A blurred frieze of cold, cool, crazy, alone, serious, angry, confused faces; in for the long haul: visionaries, bores, acolytes, poseurs, anarchists, occultists, aesthetes, theorists, spiritualists, machine-breakers, nutcases, dissemblers, prophets-in-waiting, icons, pedants.

And non-stop ecstatic pop fans – 'willing sinners' – fidgeting in Bible black, waiting in the front row for Marc Almond, singing his specially written 'Songs of Love and Murder'; actions by members of Throbbing Gristle; readings by writer and translator Paul Buck; a screening of Derek Jarman's *Sebastiane*: orgiastic martyrdom, sex and sandals, Latin subtitles
. . .

Looking up into matt darkness, tiny feeble yellow gleaming lights; then the sound of sudden emptiness, and the cold, blank, gloss-black wall briefly illuminated.

In the muffled dark, in this church of

the poisoned mind, some correlation manifests between horror and desolation; the drear landscape bares its teeth – makes itself felt, alive, in even the coarse warm fabric of the theatre seats; or the amplified acoustic gasp and sudden flash of sunlight, somehow surprising, on the muffled opening of a heavy door to the lobby.

And then we thought of Bodney Road E8 – a short road with a bend, going up to Hackney Downs; old double-fronted villas on one side, tall terraced houses on the other, their blackened yellowing brick the colour of burnt cork. Squats and drugs; houses from which the occupants never seemed to stir – facing the big estate, its tall trees in full summer leaf, lawns and windows and distant music. A strange street, as if under a spell. Curtains drawn in the middle of the hot day.

He said he went up there once to listen to 'The Man Who Sold The World', in someone's flat, and suddenly realised how far out he'd gone, how very nearly *they* got him – when the pavement seemed to rush up to his eyes, and when he cried out he couldn't hear his own voice; and there was a black woman up ahead, crossing the road, looking at him like he was mad.

Shantih shantih shantih

Docklands, 1982–'84

The water between the deserted wharves is perfectly flat, as reflective as a mirror – steel blue, then black.

Thousands of acres of scrubby nothing-ness – brittle brown wind-bent shrubs, dusty rotting concrete imprinted with the outline of railway tracks.

The ragged grey phantoms of a meaner, poorer, colder London have fled, as if at pale daybreak.

And so dogs towards the end of their lives sit patiently, and looking upwards watch the sunlight, almost alert, as though waiting to be summoned.

Kathy's rings – Hammersmith and Shaftesbury Avenue, '85–'86

The American writer Kathy Acker, then resident in Hammersmith – peroxide buzz cut, tattoos, leather jacket, muscles, bright eyes, dark lipstick – wore silver rings the size of knuckledusters.

Doubtless intended, as a style affectation, to indeed resemble knuckledusters, on closer inspection the heavy ridges of this extravagant jewellery depicted ruined and melting buildings.

'Decaying cities,' she said, sounding like Lou Reed.

We were each the city and a map of the city; with buildings and locales as events and acts and tempers – streets and districts as dialogue and characters. It felt like we walked without pause through the chapters of an autobiography, each step cumulatively writing, correcting and editing. The walked text and the written text.

New Oxford Street – a basement bar, half empty, lit the colour of pink chiffon; on the Underground platform, twin mounted television monitors show shuddering columns of dirty silver light, ceaselessly pushing across a grey void.

'Thatcher Out', 1984, '85

Bleak photographs – pictorial biopsies – told how the quickening age of electronic dance music, the springtime of postmodernism, sub-cultural lifestyle as art, fluorescent expressionist craziness, cut up and crack up, during the first half of the 1980s, occurred at, responded to, in one way or another, a time when the post-industrial urban landscape and its redundant workforce resembled the aftermath of war: ragged children, crazy rootless people, fenced-off terraces, riots, caravans in the shadow of the Westway, nowhere to go but indoors.

. . . unemployment benefits offices and their attendees; bright orange and grass-green benches against dust-coloured, litter-and-fag-butt-strewn flooring; handwritten notices and information posters on corporation off-white or putty-coloured walls. Thin doors and barred windows. A colour print of serene mountain scenery like muzak in a euthanasia suite.

Bonfires in the street; bed frame on the pavement; children in a blackened doorway, ripped and peeling posters behind them; bus stop girl in leopard print leggings, sleeveless white T-shirt and court shoes; three butchers in bloodied aprons; hoardings, scrap metal; shoulder pads.

Signing on. The people in these photographs appear stilled, bored, entombed in despondency; the offices they have to attend seem shaped to worsen, if such a thing were possible, their sense of hopelessness.

Scenes by Chekhov come to mind; that writer, physician, observer and interviewer of the sick, oppressed and displaced.

Cigarettes, stained toilet bowl, lighting tubes, greasy cooked chicken; tabloids, phalluses, lager foam, tights; all-night chemists, Lewisham rental, food wrapping, crumpled beer cans; haunted bedsits, snake murals, multiple locks, menstrual smell in empty room at silent midday.

'Slave to the rhythm': commentators in the Soho Brasserie, Old Compton Street, W1, autumn 1985

But here on the cool blue and ivory banquette, looking out over snowy white tablecloths to the evening clamour of old Soho, the times have renewed: assured glamour, evolved: adult, thinking internationally, strategically, confident, professionally – in tune with expansion, innovation. All the world an office, all the world a shop.

Barmen, white aprons, waiters, cocktails and coffee – Amaretto in heavy glasses; the creation of the espresso Martini. This assured chic is so many worlds distant from the shit basement, deafening noise, nocturnal freak and bombsite boy-*poète maudit* inhabitants of post-punk shadow – from which it is so recently descended.

The new look is 'business', sleek and clever. Is there at times a faint mist of irony, distinct yet elusive, like the scent of a new, subtle and expensive perfume?

At present it's more a feeling, a burgeoning sensibility, gathering pace. The shop as gallery, studio as business, business as studio; evolved sub-culture's open-plan office; style impresarios and analysts; branded product as art multiple and design as individualism; architecture, literature, incoming Detroit electro, new exclusivity, catwalk, image, fashion, film – introducing the outsiders to the insiders . . .

'It's Sharkey's day; it's Sharkey's day today . . .'

Last year's world of exuberantly ripped and faded denim, black broad-brimmed hats and blond highlights and headbands, perms and big T-shirts and ribbons and rags in the hair – all gone. Likewise, 'hard times chic' as pirate carnival, and post-punk softened to pantomime bagginess; horizontal black eyebrows, white bob, black polo-neck, slash red lipstick, party-time-sulky-angry-anti-Thatcher-CND-street-style . . .

Now, the new office lifestyle-style – all the world an office – and clever: toppermost of the poppermost as travels in hyper-reality, as trips to L.A.'s city of quartz. Lunch at L'Escargot, Braganza and Orso; and Manchester clubs and Tokyo technology fairs; and new furniture design and retail engineering and all the world an enterprise . . .

A vortex of evolved sub-culture, new form-alism, anatomising and interplay of image – and above all else, money.

Grace Jones at the Astoria: *'Breathe to the rhythm, work to the rhythm, love to the rhythm, slave to the rhythm . . .'*

'Discreetly Bizzare' – New Cavendish Street, W1

Meanwhile, standing as though recently tele-ported to his present position, which is at the southern end of South Molton Street, W1 (just now a highly fashionable precinct), is Stevo Pearce – charismatic founder of intention-ally misspelled Some Bizzare Records, home to Marc Almond, Cabaret Voltaire, Depeche Mode and The The, as well as new industri-alism collective Test Department and their German equivalent, Einstürzende Neubauten (oil drums of burning tar; hammered girders, scraped supermarket trolleys; 'collapsing new buildings').

Stevo looks managerial, in the new business style: somewhat portly, suited, with an air of pinstripe gangster. He appraises his location, where the West End gives way to what is still the old world opulence of Bond Street and Mayfair; as though he has indeed arrived from another planet – rather than from a first-floor office barely half a mile away, in New Cavendish Street.

The strange atmospherics of punk enabled Stevo to become a maverick visionary impresario – his roots, his musical and ideological tastes, lie deep within the Shadow-side of post-punk creativity: febrile intensity and surreal psychology; the art of the seedy, needy, desperate, violent, voyeuristic, agonised, sexual, abject and politically angry. *Soul Mining*, the first album by The The released in 1983, as much as Soft Cell's bestselling autumn '81 debut *Non-Stop Erotic Cabaret* (featuring NED Synclavier for the robot percussion and Cindy Ecstasy on backing vocals), had established the mood.

On *Soul Mining*, singer-composer Matt Johnson's vocals sound part dark-wave crooner, part tormented folk singer; these psychodynamics amplified by the distinctive cavernous boom of early '80s post-punk-pop – jangling guitars with an accordion-laced fairground swing; frantic percussion, ambient noise . . . Lyrically, the songs describe emotional insomnia, failing relationships, anxiety and dread . . . If ABC's *The Lexicon of Love* – two parts Bacharach to one part Barthes, released the previous year – had a disturbed and depressive younger brother, *Soul Mining* was it.

Time passed, hits were made (including 'What!') and money was made; Stevo – ahead of the curve – will decide to open a gallery for contemporary art, 'Discreetly Bizzare', on New Cavendish Street, W1. Fire-eaters and Thai kick-boxers will augment its grand opening.

He will pronounce at the outset, amiably enough: 'I'm not a businessman; I'm an art terrorist.'

SOUVENIR

The Berners Hotel, Berners Street, W1 –
October, 1985

Grey street outside. The afternoon grew colder.
The dusk light towards Oxford Circus is silver-
white: late sunshine under clearing cloud.

The ceiling of the vast lobby lounge of the old
Berners Hotel is ornate and complex – it might
have been borrowed from a palace. It looks
like it is made out of cinnamon sugar icing;
as though a grand tessellation of exquisitely
ridged and bordered, shallow ornamental pools,
each inset with sumptuous classical mouldings
– the house style of temperate Arcadian fantasy
– had been raised, inverted, supported upon
a deep frieze of further extravagant mouldings (winged cupid heads linked by swags of
roses), and assisted – above the tall open doors
to the dining room and bar – by a pair of
stern muscular caryatids, to face down upon
the damson carpet flecked with gold; the
marble columns on either side of the hotel's

main entrance, the somewhat shabby striped-satin sofas, wingback armchairs, glass-topped tables, ashtrays, coffee pots, monumental flower displays, small tobacconist's kiosk . . .

Beyond the lobby, facing the dark-varnished panelled Reception, a broad shallow staircase descends to dimly lit regions. Mahogany banister and cast-iron balustrade, leading to subterranean conference rooms that smell of cigarette smoke, stale coffee and carpet freshener; on a white-clothed table some unused water glasses; leaflets for a firm that runs ferries to Holland.

Here, she first saw the light of interest die in the eyes of a stranger, and that to look to the world for validation − *'How scaldingly shaming to meet myself . . .'*

Payphones, windowless cloakrooms, a single raincoat, forgotten; this long dark basement corridor; the furthest reaches . . . We wanted to say, 'The Dry Salvages' − *'I sometimes wonder if that is what Krishna meant . . .'*

Three

Borough, Elephant and Castle – February, 1986

High up, here on the fifth or sixth floor of a shabby modern building, in a big room that smells of stale cigarette smoke and cardboard, with black dust thick on the half-raised, dirty grey plastic, broken Venetian blinds.

It is late afternoon on an overcast day, nearing dusk. Time telescopes; looking down, across the point where three roads meet, we can see, just, into the windows of a first-floor office above the entrance to an Underground station. The building looks late Victorian; has a tiled entrance with a railing gateway pulled half across. Dust and litter behind the railings.

We don't know what goes on in this office. It looks as though it ought to be the city room of a small newspaper. The light inside is warm and low and yellow. It looks like they will always be working late on a winter evening that will last forever.

There was a pub around here, in a back street, and cleared waste land behind a corrugated iron fence.

We saw into these office windows again, from a halting train to New Cross, and they were the same: still working late, meeting the deadline, on a freezing winter night.

On vinyl, a sound like a recording of a sudden shout reversed. The flat white sky looked down upon the brown tarpaulin-coloured Thames.

There was a sweep of light: a photocopied sheet of radiance, a grey mist with a band of whiteness. A young man behind us listed all the records he had listened to that week and his friend was bored.

When everyone knows everything, we said in 1986, we will find a French new town and live there forever. Because what we wanted to say, to impart . . . but how to ever explain? That the late spring evening filled Wellington Street like dark warm water; and the woman's clear strong voice was full of ache and anger; and the smashing down of the microphone stand and the moaned scream.

Lloyd's of London, Lime Street, EC2 – 1986

Amstrad electronics have purchased from Sinclair Research the worldwide rights to sell and manufacture their computer products – the success of which will lead to the launch of Amstrad's market-leading PC1512 series.

Long summer evenings, 1986: Shepherd's Market alley maze, when Mayfair was half empty: the abandoned mansions, in those days, and quiet side streets like dank Venetian canals. No breeze; cigarette smoke hung in hot and stagnant air. Prostitutes with orange lipstick; slow sunset.

In the City; against night's blue, the height of its fourteen floors, its modules, metallic curves, pipes, external elevators, platforms and cranes; Deep Space Industrial: the service area depths of some vast spacecraft; like silver machine parts clamped together, with a 1925 neoclassical façade, pressed up at its base on the northwest corner – all make the new Lloyd's Building audaciously new, like Cubism was new. *'Make It new!'* An idea from which to take new bearings: a building from after modernity.

A young woman, one quiet evening, who was wearing a smart grey jersey dress, business style, and black court shoes. She was standing at the base of this new building, almost beneath it, and pressing herself, lover-like, against one of the tall wide basement windows, twice her height, that formed half the angle of a corner.

The thick glass against which she pressed her cheek, into which she gently pushed herself, eyes closed, absorbed, her hand on the thick vertical frame, was housed in lengths of grey steel; while above her turned head – blonde shoulder-length hair, straight messed fringe, as though she was hot, perspiring; a hawk-like, somewhat patrician profile – the square indentations in the cement ceiling created by the building's overhang were illuminated in silvery, turquoise light.

Empty evening City streets, in blue. A man, alone, barely glimpsed: tall, suited, owlish, short hair watered flat, severely parted, head down, hurrying. It was winter where he walked. He had done no work of the kind that augments vortices, not for months; he would return home nightly from the bank, and fall into a leaden slumber until bedtime.

Acknowledgements

The author would like to thank Lee Brackstone, Natalie Dawkins, Georgia Goodall, Lavinia Greenlaw and Antony Harwood.

Notes

Page 3: 'As my appearance . . .' – Quentin Crisp, *The Naked Civil Servant* (Flamingo, 1996)

Page 8: 'Huge office doors . . .' – John Betjeman, *Summoned by Bells* (John Murray, 1960)

Page 11: 'turning Japanese, I think . . .' – The Vapors, 'Turning Japanese', *New Clear Days* (United Artists Records, 1980)

Page 16: 'Oh baby, what . . .' – Soft Cell, 'What!', *Non Stop Ecstatic Dancing* (Some Bizzare Records, 1982)

Page 18: 'We can fall . . .' – Soft Cell, 'What!', *Non Stop Ecstatic Dancing* (Some Bizzare Records, 1982)

Page 31: 'liplicking, unzipping . . .' – ABC, 'Valentine's Day', *The Lexicon of Love* (Neutron Records, 1982)

Page 34: 'Now the world . . .' – Franz Schubert, *Winterreise*, 1827; from poems set by Wilhelm Muller

Page 34: 'Life is dark . . .' – Gustav Mahler, *Das Lied von der Erde*, 1909; setting of poem by Li Bai

Page 34: 'I don't like hiding . . .' – Public Image Ltd, 'Poptones', *Metal Box* (Virgin Records, 1979)

Page 40–41: 'This work concerned . . .' – Stephen Willats, *Cha Cha Cha* (Coracle Press, 1982)

Page 41: 'If anything happens . . .' and 'I would state . . .' – Stephen Willats, *Doppelgänger* (Actualities, 1985)

Page 42: 'We stopped in the . . .' – T.S. Eliot, *The Waste Land* (Faber & Faber, 2015)

Page 43: '. . . and drank coffee . . .' – T.S. Eliot, *The Waste Land* (Faber & Faber, 2015)

Page 43: '. . . had the tarnished . . .' – Wyndham Lewis, *Blasting and Bombardiering* (Calder, 1970)

NOTES

Page 43: 'in those days . . .' – Ezra Pound, 'Canto LXXX', *The Pisan Cantos* (New Directions, 1948)

Page 49: 'Somebody stopped the . . .' – Louis MacNeice, 'Meeting Point' (Faber & Faber, 2016)

Page 63: 'nowhere to go . . .' – Philip Larkin, 'Toads Revisited' (Faber & Faber, 1988)

Page 64: 'Well, you know . . .' – The Beatles, 'Revolution' (Apple, 1968)

Page 67: '. . . after all the sound . . .' – Jonathon Green, *All Dressed Up* (Pimlico, 1999)

Page 68: '. . . gimme little drink . . .' – Rolling Stones, 'Loving Cup', *Exile on Main St.* (Rolling Stones Records, 1972)

Page 72: 'Towards the evening . . .' – Hugh Kenner, *The Pound Era* (Pimlico, 1991)

Page 78: 'I said girl . . .' – T. Rex, 'Jeepster', *Electric Warrior* (Fly, 1971)

Page 80: 'My time is up . . .' – *Sparky's Magic Piano* (Capitol Records, 1948)

Page 82: 'and burned is . . .' – Christopher Marlowe, *Doctor Faustus* (Penguin, 1975)

Page 85: 'The "sprechgesang" . . .' – Martin Green, *Children of the Sun* (Pimlico, 1992)

Page 88: '. . . neither sad nor cheerful . . .' – André Gide, *The Immoralist* (Penguin, 1970)

Page 89: 'The rich man . . .' – E.M. Forster, *Howards End* (Penguin, 2000)

Page 90: 'Out of love for . . .' – Soren Kierkegaard, *The Kierkegaard Reader* (Fourth Estate, 1989)

Page 93–94: 'But I've got this . . .' – Prefab Sprout, 'Lions in My Own Garden (Exit Someone)' (Candle Records, 1982)

Page 106: 'Shantih . . .' – T.S. Eliot, *The Waste Land* (Faber & Faber, 2015)

Page 112: 'It's Sharkey's day . . .' – Laurie Anderson, 'Sharkey's Day', *Mister Heartbreak* (Warner Bros., 1984)

Page 113: 'Slave to the . . .' – Grace Jones, '*Slave to the Rhythm*', Slave to the Rhythm (Island Records, 1985)

Page 118: 'I sometimes wonder . . .' – T.S. Eliot, 'The Dry Salvages', *Four Quartets* (Faber & Faber, 2015)